A BLUE SHOVEL
by Robert Hershon

Hanging Loose Press

Published by Hanging Loose Press
231 Wyckoff Street
Brooklyn, N.Y. 11217

Some of these poems first appeared in the following publications: *Bird Effort, Boxspring, Chicago Review, Chowder Review, Contact II, Cottonwood Review, CrossCountry, Damascus Road, the goodly co, Handbook, Hanging Loose, Jam To-day, Midatlantic Review, Painted Bride Quarterly, Phoebe, Poetry Northwest, Poetry Now, Poetry in Public Places, Seems, Some, Sun,* and *Waves.*

Hanging Loose Press thanks the National Endowment for the Arts for grants in support of this project.

Art by Harley Elliott
Design by Larry Zirlin

ISBN 0-914610-14-7

Library of Congress Cataloging in Publication Data

Hershon, Robert.
    A blue shovel.

    I. Title.
PS3558.E79B57   811'.5'4   79-2277
ISBN 0-914610-14-7

Produced at The Print Center, Inc., Box 1050, Brooklyn, N.Y., 11202, a non-profit printing facility for literary and arts-related publications. Funded by The New York State Council on the Arts and the National Endowment for the Arts.

For Jedediah Hershon

CONTENTS

GROWING UP GROWING OLD GOING AWAY DYING

SINGING WITH FRIENDS

PACE

A BLUE SHOVEL

Growing Up Growing Old Going Away Dying

POPPEN'S LUNCHEONETTE

O God he's tried to order the breakfast special
even unto a toasted bran muffin and it's so long past eleven
God, I thought he was my friend   How the waitress grieves
how she weeps into the fluted cole slaw cups

O the sweat of the sandwich man at 12:45
That's what makes the clock go click
and the truly garnished burgers of our dreams
The hands push us through the day

Say, it's Betty from the pet shop
Yes, it's Betty from the pet shop
Why, it's Betty from the pet shop
eating dinner all alone

So   a little green check please
and your blessing   Change for the phone
and your blessing   Change for the machine
an individually wrapped
Pic-O-Mint toothpick
to begin the digging out

GROWING UP GROWING OLD
GOING AWAY DYING

These are the houses on these blocks in Flatbush which have basketball hoops affixed to their garages.

On the east side of East 29th Street, between Avenues M and L: 13 houses have no basketball hoops, 3 have. Of the latter, one has a net and one is very rusty.

On the west side of East 29th St., between Avenues L and K: 19 houses have no basketball hoops. Two houses do have hoops and both have nets. One house without a hoop has wooden supports erected, ready to hold up a backboard, and a box labeled "Superstar Backboard, Goal and Net" lying next to the garbage cans. At another house, without a hoop, a basketball lies on the ground near the back door.

East side of East 28th St., between K and J: 25 houses without hoops, 3 with, 1 net. Nothing remarkable.

West side of East 27th St., between J and L: 17 houses without hoops; one has a backboard without a hoop. Three with hoops. No nets.

East side, East 27th, between K and L: 13 houses without hoops, 2 with hoops, 3 with hoops and nets. One netless hoop very crooked.

Avenue L, north side, between East 27th and 26th Sts.: 4 houses without hoops, one with hoop and net.

West side, Bedford Ave., between L & M: 16 houses no hoops, one with hoop, one with hoop and net. One backboard barely visible over top of van in driveway; impossible to determine whether hoop and/or net in place.

South side, Avenue M, from Bedford to East 21st: 6 houses without hoops, 3 with hoops and nets, many houses without garages.

At this point, Avenue M becomes a commercial street and there are no more garages or houses. On every street surveyed, there were always more basketball hoops on the other side of the street.

A WALK: DEAD AND CLOSED

what appears to be
a bag of chicken guts
on the sidewalk is
a bag of rotten pears

the restaurant with the
"Come on in, we're open!" sign
is not always closed
only when the sign is visible

what appears to be
a dead pigeon
on the sidewalk
is probably a dead pigeon
get closer

the theater with the
"Closed for alterations
Watch for grand re-opening!" sign
will be the last building standing
as far as the eye can see

the eye is the last survivor
but you walk the next block
at your own peril

RICK'S LIQUORS

looks like any other liquor store
until you get inside and discover
that rick (rick   is that you?)
and all rick's bottles and cash
are behind plastic bullet-proof partitions
and there is no way you can get within two feet
of rick or anything that belongs to rick
we got tired of being ripped off
and locked in the can   says rick
sending your bottle down a little chute

LIKE SEAWATER

1.

in my neighborhood
during the worst of the heat
midnight looks like noon
whole families sit outside
in the dark
the men drinking beer
playing dominoes
the women talking on
the cracked steps
the babies playing
on the wet steamy sidewalks
fifty dollar cars roar
through the streets
through the jets
from the open hydrants
the gutters run as clean
as mountain streams
when it gets light
the men remain
talking quietly together
the taste of beer
in the morning
like seawater

2.

when my refrigerator was broken
i stopped at the corner store
on my way home from work
and bought two bottles of millers
knowing i could drink the first
before the second grew warm
the grocer without asking
put the bottles

14

in two separate brown bags
assuming i had a friend
waiting outside on the steps
why else would a sensible man
buy only two bottles of beer

TIN CANS

the crazy lady on the block
has a grudge against me
she claims my children
are stealing her dogs and
selling them to local butchers

late at night
she throws tin cans
into my backyard
i lie awake listening for them
one   onetwo   one   long spaces
between the crashes
each can has had the label removed
and has been carefully washed

what to do
i can't argue with a crazy lady
i can't call the police

i begin to use them
i use one as an ashtray
another to keep wooden matches in
another to measure the rainfall
another to hold old screws
i consider growing geraniums

a very satisfactory solution
i compliment myself
far better than admitting that
she has tied a tin can to my tail

A MORNING OF OLD MEN

1.

He sweeps his sidewalk every morning with the gold broom they gave him when he retired. Every morning, he asks the little girls if he can come to school with them. They consider very seriously and always say no. The first year, I walked by him quickly, eyes straight ahead. Then I glanced at him once and he nodded. Every morning now we say good morning. This morning, he mentioned arthritis. There is another old man on the next block who sits and reads the paper on his steps every morning. I am arranging to have his house condemned.

2.

Turning the corner of the furniture store with the gladiator lamps and the elephant tables, the old man and I nearly collide. His wiry moustache almost kisses my chest. Not quite. He laughs with joy. When I look back, he is still laughing. He waves. He is still waving.

3.

The Salvation Army officer in the subway sits silently by his tape recorder which plays zippy religious music for young people. Sometimes he has a tambourine. He holds it close to his ear and raps on it intently, off-beat and eager, knocking on a door, listening for footsteps.

BEER AND WINE LICENSE

McKenna at the end of the bar
empty beer mug as collection box
Dusty sunshine doesn't reach his stool

All afternoon
Gus the bartender dumps
other people's leftovers
into McKenna's glass
Lucky Lager and Burgomeister
Hamm's and Coors and Carta Blanca
sweet vermouth and burgundy
and Seven-Up and chablis

Finally McKenna's eyes begin to move
and he can lift the mug with one hand
Gus pours in a little sangria
Please   McKenna says
no cigarette butts

Which reminds Gus to
turn on the outside light

BANK SHOT FOR JOHNNY ACE

The smile of a gypsy
entering the pool room
He knows they'll all be there
and they hold his mother dear
When was it ever so warm?

Two gypsies play one-pocket
Forty gypsies are very busy
Hey   where is Johnny Ace?
Anyone seen Johnny Ace?
When was it ever so busy?

I piss on your money
and I piss on your face
says a loving cousin
Oh yeah
I piss on *your* face

No, it needed Johnny Ace
And where the hell is Johnny Ace?
We've got business We've got business
We've got business with Johnny Ace

The phone rings and the Chinese
house man calls out   Hey
it's for "any gypsy"
Was it ever all so warm?

Hey   that might be Johnny Ace
Tell the bastard we left
Give me that phone

THE LAUGH WHO WORKED

The Laugh, who worked as an Apprentice Scream, had every other Sunday off. Every other Sunday, he took the bus to Queens to visit his ancient grandmother who worked in a sweat shop, wrestling the great barrels of sweat from one end of the warehouse to the other and then back again and at her age too, tsk tsk. The grandmother also had every other Sunday off, but it was never the same Sunday that the Laugh had off, so when he got to Queens she was never there and after many visits, he began to wonder whether he really had a grandmother at all.

So the Laugh would go back and just hang around the shop and watch the Master Scream, who never took a day off, tightening a screw here and pulling out some nails there and always chipping away at something or other. Once, by an incredible coincidence, the old woman called to complain of her lot, which was filled with rats and horrible boys, but the Master explained that he didn't make service calls on Sundays, even though he couldn't remember why not. He never guessed she was the grandmother of his own apprentice, the very stuff of fiction.

Many years passed. The Laugh went into business for himself and had children of his own. He invited his grandmother to come and live with him and Peg, but she got lost on the subway and no one would help her because she was such a sweaty, bad-smelling old woman. Luckily, he found a photograph of someone else's grandmother and put it on the grand piano where it usually behaved itself, although they say on Saturday nights you could hear the screaming for blocks.

Singing With Friends

THE WRONG WAY TO REMSEN STREET

for Carol Baum

ten years ago in downtown brooklyn
a man asked me how to get to remsen street
and i gave him the wrong directions
i have regretted it ever since

i have learned to live with that guilt
    inattentive
    rushed
    selfish
    unfeeling
    deaf to a stranger's urgent need to find
    remsen street where in all probability
    a close relative lay dying
    straining to stay alive just a minute more
    long enough to whisper the combination of the safe
    to the one man the only man worthy of that trust
    the man i sent two blocks forward
    instead of two blocks back
    ten years of torment seems a small price to pay

    what i have come to question
is the assumption of faith in my own credibility
never once in these wasted shadowy years
has it occurred to me that
he might not have followed my directions
he might have checked with someone else
who sent him the right way or at least
would bear the final blame for the wrong way
which is nearly as good

actually i have assumed his faith to be unwavering
by now   walking in a straight line
he should be passing through boise idaho for the third time

covered with red leaves and seashells
every few miles he stops
rubs his feet mops his brow squints in the sun
suddenly he is filled with doubt
should he have listened to the woman
who told him to go past the bank
and make a right at burger king?
is remsen street not over the next hill?

then he puts his hat back on
and takes the first impossible step
toward pullman washington

HOW TO TURN AN OLD FUR COAT
INTO STRAWBERRY ICE CREAM

first   arrange your lumber in the shape of an amazed mouth
dance in the center   do not sing or snap your fingers
be sure the needles are sharp
you will need 13 pounds of leftover roast beef
six paper cups 11 aluminum table legs
one screen door one bottle of rubber cement
six spiders 22 yards of printed muslin
one claw hammer one cat
trace the pattern then trace the pattern again

begin to sew with mercilessly small stitches
glue your hands firmly to the wall
fill the paper cups to the brim
spill nothing
now begin to hammer
allow six days for sewing six weeks for mourning the cat
six years for hammering and removing the nails

now try on the fur coat
it is still ragged
it still smells like death
it is red now and very cold

HOW TO ACHIEVE INDEPENDENCE OF SPIRIT

on these long walks through the woods
it's a good idea to carry a few band-aids
if you cut your wrists tape your mouth
you would not want to start blubbering
and disturb the mosquitos in your teeth

train yourself to sleep through any disturbance
the sound of wet boots on the stairs
the sound of great machines shaking trees
the sound of exploding dolphins
keep these distant and indistinct
and they will not insist on being your friends

to encourage the growth of the independent spirit
all conversation is forbidden before the age of 32
the preferred opening line is ''pass the fucken ketchup''
the correct response is the stare of a person
whose nostrils are filled with shit

SINGING WITH FRIENDS

three dwarves in a barrel
how the notes do last
and the eyes do roam

these eyes
then those eyes

this splendid note
how once we all could
hit this note
now these eyes

the song always better
before it has been sung
but the singing
better than the song
and the eyes hit
this splendid note

FRIENDS OF FRIENDS

hearing them recall unknown nights of dancing
who knows what confidences they have received?
they too know where the wine glasses are
how to make the crazy stove light

year after year or two there they are
newly dead divorced living in scotland
and always looking fit
unduly familiar with our children's scars
unaware that we know about their uncles

do they know that in the desk
there are signed affadavits
stating that our friends love us better
than butterscotch pudding?
how damnably gorgeous they are

NIGHT IN RETHYMNON

my friend lights my cigarette
and the shape of the flame
is imprinted on my eye

as i look up
the shape takes its place
on the horizon

for a second or two
it's another island monster
flung down by angry gods

another layer of legend
another layer of ash

GOING NOT GOING

he isn't going to go
but if he does go
he'll be right back

he isn't going to stay
but if he does stay
it's for just a minute

if he goes
he'll drive everybody home
to walnut creek pike's peak
and mozambique

if he stays
he'll wash the dishes
the children
and the dog

he carries 200 records
in a banana box
from coast to coast
for the pleasure
of his friends

he retires early
on lumpy sofas
and always wakes refreshed

he never leaves fingerprints
on obvious surfaces

POINT PLEASANT

running back up the path
from the point
where i was looking for
the invisible sea

pursued by monsters
with hatchets
running in the tops
of the trees

at last
the solid dark of the house
heart of doorknob
i swing the door open

it presses against flesh
night rushes into my mouth

but the caveman steps
into the moonlight
and shakes my hand

we sit on the ground
hugging each other
and waiting for
civilization

MORE AND MORE THEY TALK OF GOD

what reward for their modesty
in not flying higher
than geese

they are taller than stones
and have outwitted tigers
but beavers too
will gather at the river

the admirable roaches
we have killed by the hundreds
no engraved testimonials
just heelmarks

saint gottfried of bremen
who gave a potato
to the dog

blessed saint gottfried

OBIT ENCLOSED

depend on me
to keep you up to date
on who has died

10 years since we last spoke
and even the drunken
letters have stopped

but here's someone else dead
old bill from the herald tribune
you remember old bill

i saw it in the times
thought you'd like to know
old bill died

although old bill
is not much deader to me
than you are
but i didn't see anything
about you in the times
to clip to send to someone else

nevertheless
old bill was 71
died in vermont
wife's name was louise
had three grandchildren
wrote a book once
about collecting clocks

some habits die hard
drop me a line some time
i'll be watching the obits
for you

SARAH, DO YOU THINK I'M CRAZY?

(a high school note)

"Sarah
do you think I'm crazy
or do you think Jack is a hunk?
Nod twice
if you think I'm crazy
Snap your fingers
if you agree with me"

Written in a book of
Hemingway short stories
where the women have no names

FOR LIZZIE, ON HER DISCOVERY OF 1936

yes, there was a past and it was swell
the courage of those moustaches
how sequins saved the country
you sit up till sunrise
with the lovely dead people
amazed at how well they walk and talk
then sleep all day remembering
what you're going to say tomorrow
say, that's swell
soon you'll only have to open your eyes
and they'll be dancing in your doorway

GENTLEMAN JAMES WATT TAKES THE LOCAL

my mother thought me a naughty boy
when i used her tea kettle for a toy

30 years steaming round the bend
in my brain   the whistle is the signal
to xavier cugat to play the miami beach rhumba
the band floating toward right field
a perfect peg from carl furillo
gets smiling jack smith at the plate
the notorious foxtrot dancer
screams off into the night

gentleman jack the ladies man
he can make love like no one can

and yet on a good day
i can convince myself that the train
is actually going the other way
or even standing still
passengers dancing the rhumba
through the cars
furillo firing lightbulbs
the length of the tunnel

DOUBLE RAINBOW

We stop the car
to look at the
double rainbow

Rainbow
Re-rainbow

Which are not index fingers
swizzle sticks or
quotation marks

As the car is not a cup
of coffee
or a pig jumping
the fence

Which may be banderillas
or stilts to cross the road

Which is not a tongue
or a dish towel or the way
to grandma's house

The courage of pure color
Driving past the story
and through the life

White road black
in the rain
There they go

Pace

PACE

on skinny old
lexington avenue
i speed up
to pass this man

so i can
slow down

i take
great pleasure
in the exact size
of my steps

THE CRACK-ED KNUCKLE

Unable to stop
once I learned to snap my fingers
crack my knuckles and my big toe
Even the persistent sniff
is half habit
The breathing you hear
through the keyhole
that's me
still trying to whistle
I'm working now
on a noisy wink

DISTANT NOTES

i try to capture the melody
to make it make sense
i want the tune hummable

someone is dusting a piano

FRYING

hamburgers frying
in the dark

everyone's
separate life
a mystery

TWO OLD WOMEN WHO MAY

Two old women
who may be sisters

speaking what might be
Polish on a crowded subway

Sometimes they whisper

FROM A SUNFISH

When we could no longer see the swimmers
we could still hear their voices
the father's calm instructions to his sons

FOR THE GOOD

all movies come true
the south african surgeon
requires fresh hearts
for his monster dentist
will you volunteer?
it's a painless extraction
the last thing you see
is the beautiful blue
of the surgeon's cheek
ah, the cheeks of surgeons
beautiful

SIDNEY SAYS (DO THIS)

no offense   sidney says
but who the hell needs poems
look   what can a poet tell me
about a sunset for instance
that i can't see for myself

sidney   every sunset i see now
i see your big red worried face

FOREIGN OBJECTS

do you remember the taste of your fingernails?
how carefully you chewed them into dust?
now you finger your neck and lick your lips

do you remember the taste of the eyelash?
how large it seemed in a mouthful of egg salad?
yet it was really small very small
no bigger than a train from a plane

SIX WEEKS IN A
LONG ISLAND TEACHERS LOUNGE

Mozzarella cheese is not kosher
Lots of cocker spaniels get epilepsy
We were bored to death in Puerto Rico

We were bored to death in Puerto Rico
Lots of cocker spaniels get epilepsy
Mozzarella cheese might be kosher

MACHO MADNESS

the exquisite summer pleasure
of pissing a mosquito to death

THIRD WEEK

not a thought of you all morning
then a blue car turns the corner

crash

SLEEPLESS ALONE

who's that breathing heavy
waking me up

me

who's that crashing around
waking me up

me

whose hand is that

mine

STILL THERE

Can't you ever be on time
I've been standing on this corner
amusing myself by mistaking
the ugliest people the clumsiest people
for you   the spitting images

POPULARITY

1.

I could hardly wait to get to the party!
I had news of the death of everyone's best friend!

2.

God was I funny I was terrific
I wanted the words to spin so fast
everything would stand still
I wanted to tear off their faces
and spit in their blood

A Blue Shovel

MAY COMMA MERRY MONTH OF

now you take your mayfly
lives just one day
born without a mouth or a stomach
or some such, gets no nourishment
and it might not be a nice day
maybe that one day
is in troy ny in the snow
and in mayfly eternity
if somebody asked
what's it all about anyway
a representative sample of mayflies
would say: troy ny in the snow

now i was born in may
and in my lifetime maypoles have disappeared
and parades have given way to drowning sailors
and maybe this isn't going to work out
maybe every sailor drowns every time
maybe the mayflies will forget memorial day
they'll scratch their tiny heads
and say what what who

it's true mayflies are also called june bugs
this argues for second chances for hanging on
coming in on a wing and a prayer
and maybe everything will work out
but there are no julyflies

THE SCAPESNAKE IN THE SNAKESCAPE

One of the boys said:
maybe it crawled away
after it died

All-night search
in the woods
Hardware merchants
in hip boots
The eyes of the dogs
First light steaming

How sharper than a serpent's
tooth, we often laughed
snakehipping through
piles of dirty linen

One of the boys said:
maybe it crawled away
after it died

But we weren't sure
It might be hiding
in the shower or coiled
around the butter dish

We could try it out
When the men return at midnight
tired bones stirring black
coffee   we'll try to look
properly sad for the photographers
a great loss/a brave effort
have a donut

Then we'll dance through the house
all night   the dance of the freedom
of the heavy boots

Have a donut
Take two
they're small

One moved

TO A TURN

15 years sleeping together
now i anticipate your elbow
in my stomach
dead asleep
but i know the moves
you too
you know when the knee is coming
15 years
we still hit out
it's the turning we've learned

FLUFFY PUFFY TUFFY

A sensible child will always
name a kitten Frisky

Fluffy Puffy Tuffy Muffy
Pinky or Mr. Stripes

This ensures that
in the middle of the night
the cat
willfully or screaming
will not turn into
a pickup truck

Thus our careful endearments

THE FAMOUS CAT

the famous cat
looks out
the famous window

drawings of
outraged pigs
on our swampy
bed

eating an apple
like war

anagrams of
my name
mania of puzzlers
by mothlight

hot colors
loss of benefits

in an orange room
i write
a deadly letter

the famous cat
sits on
the famous stove

EXTENSIVE DISCOURAGEMENT

To express the extent of your discouragement
you spend all week watching Hockey Highlights
and scraping carrots until there is nothing left
but curly orange garbage up to your knees
The little grey men with the sharp blades
move very fast but out of focus
skating off the edges of the picture
At what point does the carrot
cease to be a carrot

To dramatize the prevailing hopelessness
I leave all the doors open at night
as an invitation to burglars
optimistic carrot-chasers
with ambitious goals and simple plans

They keep the appointment
little hockey players kicking out into the dark
They take the cash but not the credit cards
They have no patience with middle-men
To demonstrate their subtlety
they take all my shoes and underwear
and do not murder us this time

THE THIRD OF JULY

don't let my father die of a heart attack
or your children drown in the river
or my children throw themselves in front of trucks
or all these houses turn into roman candles
don't let your silly car disintegrate five miles outside town
or the russians attack new york harbor in ironclad sailboats
don't let the phone ring anymore with people looking for
                                     bowling alleys
please don't break a leg or get a toothache
i am sitting here hugging myself to ward off leprosy and the flu
couldn't everyone go home and be quiet for 71 hours
71 hours
i've never actually counted hours before
they're huge they fill the room dead bears
i'll type this again and again
70 hours
i just want to see you walk through a door
and know that you are looking for me/amazing amazing there
                                     she is
and all the words from movie ads are restored to life
incredible astounding unbelievable amazing amazing
outside the kids can't wait for tomorrow
they light up the streets with their blockbusters
whistle chasers and silver jets
how did they know!

THE FIFTH OF JULY

it was the second coldest second rainiest
fourth of july ever said the man with the radar
nearly a record all celebrations were cancelled
but i am an american i believe in progress
just desserts ladders of success
i believe that if i climb up right this minute
and go sit at a bar in kansas or maine
and stare at the door hard enough
sooner or later you'll come rushing in
and be there with me
because that would be better
and things are supposed to keep getting better
not blow up in my hands this way

is there a chance for you and me? no
is there a chance for you and me? no
i am an american i believe in holidays
i believe in anniversaries and coincidence
just a year ago today i first held you in the morning
i am an american i believe in neatness
is there a chance for you and me? no
is there a chance for you and me? no
i'm an american student i learn by rote
is there a chance for you and me? no

a man in the bar is furious at the government
for changing the date of veterans day
as though he'd celebrated the armistice in 1918
as though long weekends were calculated betrayals
but they wouldn't mess with the goddamn fourth he said
only a few drunks out in the rain last night
trying to get the spark to catch
not understanding the day had slipped away

i tried to wedge myself into your life
you pulled yourself taut and sent me shooting out
i am an american i believe in targets
i believe in progress
i believe in fallacious concepts of romantic love
i believe in sociologically bankrupt theories
of cinematic inevitability i believe in movies
as anaesthesia i believe in whiskey for pain
i believe in testimony by anecdote:
harold ross's favorite reporter resigned
from the new yorker to go to hollywood
ross was overcome all he could say was
god bless you mcnulty god damn it

I BELIEVE MYSELF TO BE EARNEST

when i wake up in the morning
i think it's the middle of the night
when i wake up in the middle of the night
i think the sun is burning the curtains
i am awake and answering questions
of no consequence except life and death
i believe myself to be earnest
but at noon the moon is still high

HERE'S A SURPRISE

here's a surprise
you and me in your bright little house

and here's a surprise
you and me in your cheery bed

o you are a prize in the morning

YOU LIKE GETTING LETTERS

You like getting letters
I like writing letters
Ain't that lucky
This is a letter
Just reach out and take it
No sense being 10 states apart
I'll just sit up in bed
and write this letter
and hand it to you
You can add some footnotes
back talk headlines lip synch
toe jam tooth sense butt right in
and hand it back
It's a whole new class of mail
Will it be popular

CATS AND DOGS

for Jean Stewart

did you hear that
did you hear that
cats and dogs
cats and dogs
creeping up
on the house

did you hear that
cats and dogs
dance in the leaves
very slow
very quiet
cats and dogs
in the dark
dancing slow

did you feel that
cats and dogs
knock on the windows
cats and dogs
knock on the doors
cats and dogs singing slow
in the moonlight
cats and dogs low voices
in the dark light
and here they are
cats and dogs
knock on the door
cats and dogs
walking slow
through the halls
and here they are

here they are
on the bed
cats and dogs
warm your feet
cats and dogs
hold your hand
cats and dogs
stroke your hair
cats and dogs
singing in your ear
the tune that was on
the tip of your tongue
cats and dogs
walk up and down
walk up and down
your sweet body
that tender weight
that just-right weight

cats and dogs
stay all night
sleep slow
cats and dogs
in morning sun
slow morning
cats and dogs
look in your eyes
good morning
they left their bags
and their bones
and their toys
just outside

in the slow
morning
they'll stay
for lunch
they'll stay
for tea
they'll stay
for brandy and biscuits
and
did you hear that
they're singing again

A BLUE SHOVEL

at three o'clock this morning
i became obsessed with the idea
that no one ever thinks about me
unless i am standing right in front of her/him/them
which is why i have to do it all myself
and never have time left over for composing oratorios

i put this theory to certain proofs
first, i counted to 1,060 fifteen times and the phone
didn't ring even once   then i called 49 people
selected scientifically to include a full range of
very close friends and people i went to grover cleveland high
                                          school with
and not one of them said: hey, i was just thinking about you

                    that list (he paused dramatically, the audience
shifted in their seats and coughed nervously) that list
included several people in this very room
        (again the audience stirred, there were groans: o my god
        in the back of the room a man rose from his seat
        then saw the door was guarded)
well, i want you to know i forgive you
it may not even have been your fault
i may have been giving off fumes of some sort that induced amnesia
so that no sooner would i finish saying
the matisse drawing i bought for you is in the next room, i'll just
                                          get it
than you would be thinking who was that masked man? why is
                                          that curtain rustling?
what was i going to do with these eggs?

so i'm changing everything
i'm going to be quieter looser denser taller faster closer to cold water
than a blue shovel tighter noisier dancing the new steps two three
various touchstones will be skimmed across the lake
so the last time you heard me tell you
about my being the only person you'll meet this year
who has been the guest of honor at a rotary club luncheon
in valdese, north carolina, a town founded by descendants
of the waldensian heresy who have all become manufacturers of
                                                        pantyhose
was the last time   except for this time
and there's always just a hint of a written excuse from the
                                              family doctor
for this time: please excuse his absence from your presence
he's always been difficult to envision in a particular place
at any rate, the doors are still barricaded
so you might as well get a head start on memorizing my life's work
i'll wait till you're through i'll just stand right here

LAST NIGHT THE WIND CAME IN

last night the wind came in
last night the wind came in
it blew through the room
it turned the pages of the book
it blew the socks off the table ·
it blew the sheets away
it blew the light bulbs out
it blew the cat's whiskers off
it blew the laces out of the boots
it blew the wives out of the beds
it blew the children out of their childhoods
it blew the buttons out of the buttonholes
it blew the letters out of the envelopes
it blew the skin off the places near the bone
last night the wind came in
it blew the pictures out of the frames
it blew the roses out of the cheeks
it blew the keys off the typewriter
it blew the rings off the fingers bells off the toes
it blew upstairs and downstairs
through the keyholes and the cracks in the walls
it left everything leaning one way or another
it blew through the grease in the oven
and the ice in the freezer
it blew over the place of the horrible
realization and the place of the bitter recrimination
and the place of the decision to try to get out
it bent the toothbrush bristles this way
and the hairbrush bristles that way
it blew the bodies out of these arms
and into those arms
last night the wind came in
it blew the arms all over the room

it blew the eyes to rolling wildly
it blew the hairs off the body
it left everything shivering and unsure
it rose and it fell and it doubled back
and it didn't miss a corner or a turn
and in the morning
the wind came in
and it blew away the daytime
and it blew away up and down
and it blew away hot and cold in and out
far and near good and bad sooner and later
it blew away these words these voices
it left the sound of itself
the whisper and the promise
and the certainty of wind